ZOO ANIMALS

by Sandy Cortright

Illustrated by Marilee Carroll

BARRON'S

New York • London • Toronto • Sydney

All inquiries should be addressed to:
Barron's Educational Series, Inc.
250 Wireless Boulevard
Hauppauge, New York 11788

Library of Congress Catalog Card No. TK
International Standard Book No. 0-8120-4436-3

Library of Congress Cataloging-in-Publication Data

Cortright, Sandy.
    Zoo animals/by Sandy Cortright; illustrated by Marilee Carroll.
    p.   cm.
    Summary: Presents facts about a variety of zoo animals, from the
American alligator to Grant's zebra.
    ISBN 0-8120-4436-3
    1. Zoo animals — Juvenile literature. [1. Zoo animals.
2. Animals.] I. Carroll, Marilee, ill. II. Title.
QL77.5.C67   1990   90-56
596-dc20   CIP
                                     AC

PRINTED IN HONG KONG
0123 9923 987654321

INTRODUCTION

Going to the zoo can be a wonderful experience, especially if you know some facts about the animals. This book will answer questions you might have about what you'll see. Open your eyes, and you might be surprised!

Can you guess what kind of a sound each animal makes? Sometimes it's a squeak and sometimes it's a loud roar.

Look at what the animals eat. A bunch of leaves might taste as good as ice cream to some animals. Would you like to eat with them?

Watch the mothers take care of their young. Does baby get a ride on her back? Where do they sleep? Some stand; others roll up in a nest.

The information gathered in this book came from animal keepers, docents (zoo guides), and books about animals.

Not all animals are in all zoos. Try to see how many are in the zoo you visit. Remember, too, that if you take the time to watch each animal, you'll see things that will make your visit even more exciting.

AFRICAN LION

HOME: Open plains and scrub forests of Africa.

LIFE SPAN: 15 years in the wild; 15 to 30 years in the zoo.

LOOKS: The head and body are 8 feet long. The male lion can weigh as much as 500 pounds — about the same as the weight of three grown men. The females are smaller. Lions have short hair; only the male has a long hairy collar (mane). The hind legs are strong for pouncing as much as 12 feet in a single bound. Lions have good hearing and eyesight. The roar of a lion can be heard for over 5 miles.

BABIES: One to six spotted cubs are born in a litter, just like kittens. They stay close to the mother for 18 to 24 months.

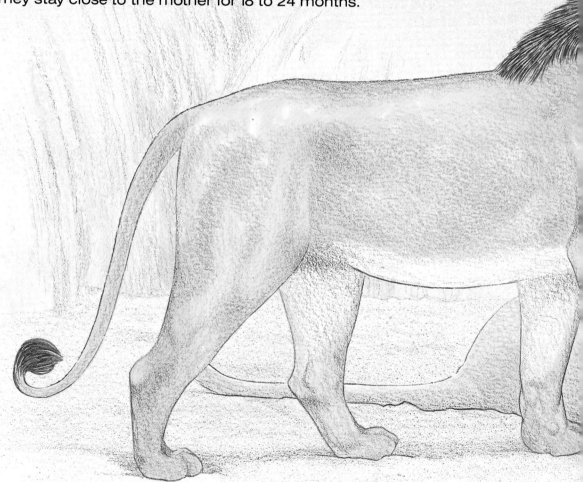

FOOD: Lions eat any kind of meat. Their favorites are zebra, wildebeest, impala, and antelope. Sometimes they steal food from hyenas.

HABITS: A group or "pride" of lions consists of a single male, several females, and their babies. Lions sleep most of the day and hunt at night. Females are the hunters and males are the protectors of the pride. Lions eat only every 4 or 5 days and can eat as much as 30 to 40 pounds of meat and skin in large gulps. They don't chew their food like we do.

BENGAL TIGER

ENDANGERED SPECIES

HOME: Jungles and forests of Asia.

LIFE SPAN: 15 years in the wild; 20 in the zoo.

LOOKS: A full-grown male Bengal tiger's body can grow to 9 feet long and have a 3 foot long tail (this is as long as a car). Their weight can be 500 pounds or more. The females are smaller. Tigers are the largest of the cat family. The fur is short and dense. No two tigers have the same pattern of stripes, just as people have different fingerprints. Large eyes and good hearing help them hunt for food. Their jaws are powerful, with large canine teeth for tearing meat.

BABIES: Usually one to four cubs are born to a litter. The birth weight is 2½ to 3 pounds, about the same as a small house cat. Cubs open their eyes between 2 and 3 weeks of age. By 7 months, cubs can kill for themselves.

FOOD: Deer, wild pigs, young buffalo, young elephants, birds, fish, small mammals, and dead animals.

HABITS: A tiger likes to live alone. In a single year it can kill as many as 50 deer. These big cats are good swimmers and enjoy bathing on warm days. While hunting, tigers follow their prey and slowly sneak up on it. When near enough, they pounce on the unsuspecting animal and kill it in an instant.

CHEETAH

ENDANGERED SPECIES

HOME: Savannas and plains of India, west through Africa.

LIFE SPAN: 12 years in the wild; up to 17 years in the zoo.

LOOKS: The cheetah weighs 100 or more pounds. Its head is small, with tear-shaped markings on the face.

BABIES: A litter has two to five cubs. The birth weight is 8½ to 9 ounces.

FOOD: Hoofed animals, rabbits, ostriches, and smaller birds.

HABITS: The cheetah is the fastest land mammal, running as fast as a car, up to 70 miles per hour for short distances.

LEOPARD

ENDANGERED SPECIES

HOME: Forests, bush, rocky hillsides, or savannas of southern Asia and most of Africa.

LIFE SPAN: 12 years in the wild; 24 in the zoo.

LOOKS: An adult male can weigh as much as 180 pounds. The coat has black spots in the shape of circles.

BABIES: One to three cubs are born blind and helpless, just like kittens.

FOOD: Any animal it can catch.

HABITS: To keep other predators from stealing its kill, the leopard stores it in the branches of a tall tree.

GRAY WOLF OR TIMBER WOLF

HOME: Forests and wilderness areas of North America, Europe, and Asia.

LIFE SPAN: 8 to 16 years in the wild; 20 years in the zoo.

LOOKS: The male's weight can be as much as 165 pounds; about the same as a grown man. The females are smaller. The fur is heavy for protection from the cold.

BABIES: A litter of five to six cubs is born. They are blind and totally dependent, just like newborn puppies.

FOOD: Hoofed animals and small animals.

HABITS: The wolves live in packs of 5 to 25 members, similar to a large human family, with cousins, uncles, aunts, grandparents, parents, brothers, and sisters.

ARCTIC FOX

HOME: Treeless tundra to coastal mountains of Alaska, Canada, Asia, and Europe.

LIFE SPAN: 6 years in the wild; 13 years in the zoo.

LOOKS: The Arctic fox is as long as a 30-inch baseball bat and weighs between 10 and 15 pounds. The long, thick fur is white to cream-colored in winter and gray to yellow in summer. This helps it blend with its surroundings.

BABIES: In late spring a litter of five to eight cubs is born. The male helps care for the babies.

FOOD: Birds, small animals, fish, eggs, reindeer calves, berries, and dead animals.

HABITS: Arctic foxes live in groups and hunt together. They follow polar bears and feed on the leftovers from their meals.

AMERICAN BLACK BEAR

HOME: Wooded areas of North America from northern Mexico to Alaska.

LIFE SPAN: 25 to 30 years.

LOOKS: The smallest bear in North America is also the most common. Its weight is between 300 and 500 pounds. The smooth, short coat can vary in color from black to cinnamon. In the fall, bears are larger because they've eaten lots of food all summer to keep them nourished all winter.

BABIES: Two or three cubs are born in January, weighing about as much as a giant tube of toothpaste. They are blind and deaf at birth, with little hair. The cubs drink mother's milk until they are big enough to leave the den.

FOOD: Berries, fruit, ants, fish, mice, squirrels, grasses, birds, and dead animals.

HABITS: Bears are good tree climbers and can run fast. The males live alone. Their dens are made under fallen logs or in caves. In winter bears sleep but do not hibernate. They don't eat until spring.

POLAR BEAR

ENDANGERED SPECIES

HOME: Snow- and ice-covered regions of the Arctic Circle.

LIFE SPAN: 20 to 35 years.

LOOKS: One of the largest of the bears, the male averages 1400 pounds and the female weighs about 800 pounds. The polar bear's body has adapted to life on ice or swimming in freezing water. It has a layer of fat under the skin and powerful legs. Wide, flat paws with fur-covered soles keep its feet warm. The fur is thick and oily to keep the body from freezing. Its sense of hearing and smell helps it find food.

BABIES: The mother gives birth to hairless and blind twin cubs in the winter. They weigh 1 or 2 pounds each, about the size of a small melon. By spring the cubs weigh 15 pounds and are developed enough to leave the den.

FOOD: Seals, birds, vegetation, and fish.

HABITS: The polar bear is a strong swimmer. The female lives on land when she has her babies. Polar bears do not seem to fear human beings. They can run up to 25 miles per hour and can swim 6 miles per hour.

GIANT PANDA

ENDANGERED SPECIES

HOME: Bamboo forests in the high mountains of China and Tibet.

LIFE SPAN: 25 years in the zoo.

LOOKS: The giant panda looks like a bear but is related to the raccoon. Pandas have a black and white woolly fur. The head and body measure 6 feet long, and the body weight is up to 300 pounds, about the same as an American black bear. The teeth and jaws are strong for chewing bamboo.

BABIES: At birth cubs weigh 4 or 5 ounces, about the size of a pat of butter. The eyes open at 6 weeks. Panda mothers are very gentle and carry the babies for the first few weeks.

FOOD: Bamboo shoots and occasionally small birds, rats, and snakes.

HABITS: The panda is becoming hard to find in the wild. It feeds at night and is difficult to see. Pandas live alone. There are probably fewer than 1000 pandas living in the wild. Only a few live in zoos. The World Wildlife Fund uses the panda as their symbol.

SPOTTED HYENA

HOME: Plains and mountains of Africa.

LIFE SPAN: Up to 35 years.

LOOKS: Doglike in appearance, the hyena weighs up to 180 pounds; females are smaller. Its length is 4 to 5½ feet plus a short tail. A large head with its front legs longer than its back legs gives the hyena an unusual walk. The neck muscles are well developed, and the teeth are strong for chewing bones.

BABIES: One or two offspring are born with their eyes open. The babies can walk and run soon after birth.

FOOD: Hyenas hunt zebra, wildebeest, and any other animal they can catch.

HABITS: Hyenas are night hunters. They can run short distances at 40 miles per hour. Lions frighten hyena packs away from a kill, and the hyena waits to eat the leftovers. The hyena is a shy animal and hides from human beings.

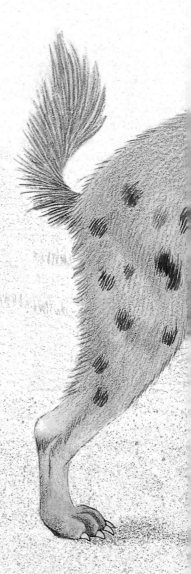

HARBOR SEAL

COMMON SEAL

HOME: Coastal waters and shores in the northern parts of the world.

LIFE SPAN: 40 years.

LOOKS: The seal measures up to 5½ feet long and weighs up to 250 pounds. There are no outside ears. The back flippers cannot be turned forward to lift the body when the seal is out of water.

BABIES: The pup is covered with a soft white wool coat at birth. The mother teaches the pup to swim and catch fish.

FOOD: Fish.

HABITS: A harbor seal can swim underwater for up to 20 minutes. It has been known to swim great distances up rivers following fish.

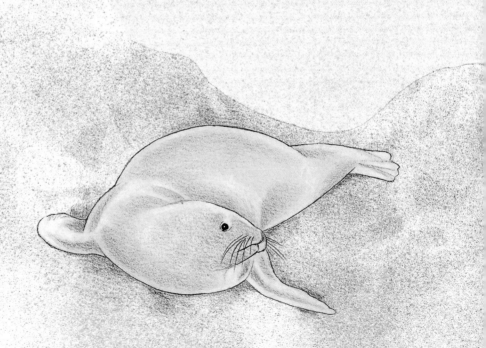

CALIFORNIA SEA LION

HOME: Islands, either rocky or sandy spots, off the Pacific Coast of North America.

LIFE SPAN: 20 to 23 years in the zoo.

LOOKS: The male California sea lion weighs up to 600 pounds; females weigh 200 pounds. The ears are small, but hearing is good. They make a loud barking sound.

BABIES: A single pup is born weighing 12 to 14 pounds; it looks like a loaf of French bread. At about 1 month of age the pup learns to swim.

FOOD: Squid, octopus, and fish.

HABITS: Sea lions can swim 10 miles an hour. The front flippers are used to pull themselves through the water; the back flippers steer.

RING-TAILED LEMUR

ENDANGERED SPECIES

HOME: Dry country along rivers in Madagascar.

LIFE SPAN: 20 years.

LOOKS: The head and body measure 18 inches, about the same size as a house cat. It has an extra long tail, too. The face has eye rings, a black-tipped nose, and muzzle. The cheeks and forehead are white. The eyes face forward. The soft body fur is gray. The long narrow feet have a big toe that can grasp things the way you use your thumb. The soles of the feet are as smooth as shoe leather.

BABIES: A new baby's weight is between 1½ and 2½ ounces, about the same as a letter. The well-developed baby clings to its mother's belly for the first few weeks. When it gets older, it rides on her back.

FOOD: Fruit and insects.

HABITS: Ring-tailed lemurs stay together in troops of 10 to 20 members that are lead by females. On the ground they hold their tails high so everyone can see them. Feeding is usually early in the morning or in late afternoon. Food is held in the front paws when eating. In the evening the troop moves to the trees for sleeping.

SPIDER MONKEY

HOME: Tropical forests from southern Mexico to Brazil.

LIFE SPAN: 20 or more years in the zoo.

LOOKS: The spider monkey is known for its long legs and grasping tail. The hair is coarse and stringy.

BABIES: The babies are totally dependent for 6 months. When the baby rides on its mother's back, it wraps its tail around hers to hold on.

FOOD: Vegetation, insect larvae, and tree snails.

HABITS: Spider monkeys live in social groups. They spend most of their time leaping from tree to tree in search of food.

BLACK AND WHITE COLOBUS MONKEY

ENDANGERED SPECIES

HOME: Tropical and high mountain rain forests of Africa.

LIFE SPAN: 20 years in the wild; up to 29 years in the zoo.

LOOKS: Males weigh about 25 pounds; females are smaller. The body is black with a head crest, whiskers, a long fringed "cape," and a tail of white fur. It has no cheek pouches.

BABIES: The single offspring is born helpless. The mother must feed and carry it for 2 weeks before it can cling to her belly.

FOOD: Leaves and shoots.

HABITS: Colobus monkeys live in trees and rarely come to the ground. When alarmed they make a loud barking sound.

GIBBON

Siamang

HOME: Rain forests of Southeast Asia.

LIFE SPAN: 25 to 30 years.

LOOKS: Both adult male and female weigh about 20 to 25 pounds. The fur is black and the throat sac is gray. The siamang is the largest of the gibbon family.

BABIES: The siamang gives birth to a single offspring. It clings to the mother's fur for the first few weeks.

FOOD: Fruit, leaves, and occasionally eggs, birds, and insects.

HABITS: They spend 9 to 10 hours a day feeding in the trees. When threatened, they fill the throat sac or pouch with air and scream. The gibbon is a great acrobat.

COMMON CHIMPANZEE ENDANGERED SPECIES

HOME: Rain forest, woodland, and savanna of western and central Africa.

LIFE SPAN: 40 years in the wild; 60 years in the zoo.

LOOKS: The weight of adults ranges from 80 to 190 pounds, about the same weight as a human being. The body is covered with thick hair that protects them from the rain. There is little hair on the face. The chimpanzee has four times the strength of a human being.

BABIES: The offspring need to be cared for by their mothers for 2 years. They must learn how to gather food.

FOOD: Leaves, shoots, bark, seeds, insects, fish, and small animals.

HABITS: Chimpanzees live in groups that are comfortable living in trees or on the ground, moving with the food supply.

LOWLAND GORILLA

ENDANGERED SPECIES

HOME: Lowland rain forest of Africa.

LIFE SPAN: 35 years in the wild; 50 in captivity.

LOOKS: The male lowland gorilla can weigh 500 pounds or more; females are smaller. When standing on feet and knuckles, they measure 4 to 6 feet tall. The arm span can reach 6 feet or more.

BABIES: The offspring weigh 4 to 5 pounds, about the size of a bag of sugar. Infants are dependent on their mothers for food and grooming for the first few months.

FOOD: Vines, berries, thistles, leaves, bark, and insects.

HABITS: Gorillas live on the ground and walk on all fours, supporting their bodies on their knuckles. They live in small social groups led by a male called a silverback. Most of their day is spent looking for food or napping. Late in the afternoon they build a nest on the ground or on low tree branches. When disturbed, they beat their chests. Gorillas can run on their hindlegs when fleeing danger or threatening an enemy.

ASIAN OR INDIAN ELEPHANT

ENDANGERED SPECIES

HOME: Dense jungle, tropical forests, grasslands, and dry woodlands of India and Southeast Asia.

LIFE SPAN: 60 years in the wild; 70 to the zoo.

LOOKS: Males weigh 5 to 6 tons, about the size of a school bus. Females are smaller. Their backs have a high curved shape. The forehead is high and rounded. The ears are small and triangular in shape. Only the males have tusks that show. The skin is smooth and marked with pink spots. The trunk has one "finger" at the end for picking up objects, such as fruit.

BABIES: A baby weighs 220 pounds at birth. Calves suckle with their mouths.

FOOD: Fruit, grasses, reeds, bamboo, and other plants.

HABITS: Elephants in the wild spend 18 to 20 hours a day eating and can drink 50 gallons of water. That's enough to fill two bathtubs to the top! They bathe themselves in rivers and can spray a shower from their trunks to cool themselves. Rolling in mud protects the skin from insects. In the jungle, elephants help other animals by making trails. Elephants are not frightened of mice.

AFRICAN ELEPHANT

ENDANGERED SPECIES

HOME: Grassy plains, forests, and savannas of Africa.

LIFE SPAN: 60 years in the wild; 70 in the zoo.

LOOKS: The largest land mammal weighs 10,000 to 12,000 pounds and stands as tall as a large dump truck. An African elephant has a flat forehead, with large ears that are used as a fan for cooling its body. Both males and females have tusks. The trunk has two "fingers" on the end for grasping small items. Food and water can be sucked up and put into the mouth by the trunk. An elephant has six sets of molars (teeth). They lose them just like you lose your baby teeth. The African elephant has four toes on each foot but only three toenails.

BABIES: A calf weighs 200 to 260 pounds at birth. Within 2 days it can walk with the herd.

FOOD: An adult eats one to several hundred pounds of plants and 40 or more gallons of water daily.

HABITS: Herds are led by an old cow (female). An elephant can run 24 miles an hour for short distances. Communication varies from a loud trumpet call to a squeaking sound.

BLACK RHINOCEROS

ENDANGERED SPECIES

HOME: Forests with open clearings, scrub, and forested savannas, always near water, in Africa.

LIFE SPAN: 50 years.

LOOKS: The adult black rhino is 10 to 12 feet long, about the size of a large station wagon. Its weight can be as much as 2500 pounds. Two horns, which are actually tightly packed hairs, are close together on the nose. Their eyesight is so poor that rhinos run into bushes and trees. Their hearing and sense of smell are good.

BABIES: A calf weighs 70 pounds at birth. It stays with its mother until about 3½ years of age.

FOOD: Shoots and twigs of mimosa and other woody, thorny bushes.

HABITS: Behavior is unpredictable and unsociable. When the rhino sees a stranger, it charges, running 20 to 35 miles an hour. Then it lowers its head, striking with its horn. During the heat of the day it stretches out on one side or bathes in cooling swamps. By covering its body with mud it gets relief from parasites. Poachers hunt the black rhino for its horns, which are used in Oriental folk medicine to cure sickness, or for dagger handles.

GRANT'S ZEBRA

HOME: Grassy plains and savannas of East Africa.

LIFE SPAN: 25 years in the wild; 29 in the zoo.

LOOKS: The Grant's zebra is the smallest of the three species found in the south of Africa. It is the size of a small horse. No two zebras have the same pattern of stripes. They are different, just like people. A fully grown zebra weighs up to 750 pounds. Its legs are short and the body is stocky. The striped mane is neat and the tail is tufted. Grant's zebra has broader stripes than other kinds of zebras.

BABIES: A zebra foal (baby) weighs 65 to 75 pounds at birth. It has a short body and long legs and can walk shortly after birth just like a pony.

FOOD: Tall, coarse grasses.

HABITS: Zebras eat grass in the early morning or late afternoon. They sleep standing up, and the herds walk with antelope, wildebeest, ostrich, kudu, and giraffe. They move to new grasslands when the food runs out. Zebras can have bad tempers and be dangerous. When alarmed they make a loud braying sound ending in a whinny like a horse. When running from danger, zebras can reach a speed of 50 miles per hour for short distances. The lion is their greatest enemy.

COMMON (NILE) HIPPOPOTAMUS

HOME: River areas with grassland and marshes of Africa.

LIFE SPAN: 35 years in the wild; 45 in the zoo.

LOOKS: The hippo is 12 to 15 feet long and weighs 2500 to 5000 pounds, about the size of a car. Its color is dark brown with pink around the mouth and eyes. The lower incisors (teeth) are used for clipping grass, and the upper tusks are used for fighting. The skin is thick and rough, with almost no hair. The skin glands make a red oil to keep the hide moist. A hippo's eyes, ears, and nose are raised so that the hippo can see, hear, and breathe while the rest of its body is under water. Each foot has four toes.

BABIES: Usually a single calf is born weighing 60 to 100 pounds. Birth may be under water. The baby swims immediately and can even nurse there.

FOOD: Grass and aquatic plants.

HABITS: Herds are made up of 10 to 30 females and offspring. Bulls live alone or form groups outside the herds. Hippos spend most of the day in the water and feed on land at night.

WARTHOG

HOME: Savannas, light forests, and bush of Africa.

LIFE SPAN: 10 to 18 years.

LOOKS: An adult warthog is about the same size as a domestic pig. Its weight can be about 165 to 300 pounds. Males have 10 to 25 inch canine teeth or tusks; females have 6 to 10 inch tusks. The eyes are higher on the head and farther back than in other kinds of pigs. Warts are located on the sides of the head in front of eyes. Large calluses are on the wrists or knees.

BABIES: A litter of two to seven (usually three) piglets is born in an underground den, each weighing 1½ to 2 pounds, about the same as a large jar of peanut butter. They stay with the mother for nearly a year.

FOOD: Grass, roots, berries, bark of young trees, and sometimes dead animals.

HABITS: Warthogs are active during the day. They like to find ready-made homes, such as abandoned aardvark dens — a protected place to have their babies. If frightened or seeking safety, the adult enters the den last by backing into the opening. When feeding, the warthog drops to its wrists or knees to graze. The tail is limp like a rope while grazing, but it stands straight up when frightened or running.

BACTRIAN CAMEL

HOME: Dry grassy plains and desert regions of the Gobi Desert in China.

LIFE SPAN: 45 to 50 years.

LOOKS: The Bactrian camel has two humps on its back where fat is stored. Camels have long legs and broad, cushioned feet that have tough, spongy soles. This helps them walk on hot sand.

BABIES: The offspring can walk within hours after birth. The calf stays with its mother until it is 4 years old.

FOOD: Any plants, dried shrubs, or thorns.

HABITS: A camel can drink 30 gallons of water in only 10 minutes. It changes this water to fat, which is stored in the hump.

ARABIAN CAMEL OR DROMEDARY

HOME: Dry and desert regions of North Africa or the Middle East.

LIFE SPAN: 45 to 50 years.

LOOKS: The Arabian camel has long eyelashes to protect the eyes from blowing dust and sand. This kind of camel has only one hump on its back.

BABIES: A calf is born between January and March. It stays with its mother for 4 years.

FOOD: Plants, thorns, and scrub brush.

HABITS: Arabian camels can travel nearly 100 miles in 1 day with no food or water. The hump stores water as fat and energy.

LLAMA

HOME: High plateaus of South America.

LIFE SPAN: 20 years.

LOOKS: The llama looks like a camel but without a hump. It has a small head, large eyes, a split upper lip, and a long neck. Its hair is short on the head, neck, and legs, with long, thick wool on the rest of the body. Llamas grow to 5 to 6 feet long from head to tail and weigh from 150 to 300 pounds.

BABIES: A baby is called a calf. It is able to run soon after birth. By 12 weeks it is weaned.

FOOD: Grasses.

HABITS: The llama has been domesticated for thousands of years and has been used as a beast of burden. Clothes are made from its woolly hair. When annoyed or threatened, the llama spits and bites. Known for being surefooted and able to live at high levels in the mountains, it is also a good swimmer.

AXIS DEER OR CHITAL

HOME: Open grassland to bamboo forests and light jungle, usually near a stream with a ravine for shelter in India or Ceylon.

LIFE SPAN: 10 to 15 years.

LOOKS: The axis deer is small. Its body is about the length of a bike. Its weight is 60 to 100 pounds. The coat is coarse. The coloring varies from bright reddish brown to yellowish brown. Spots of white are on its back and neck, with white on the underparts and inside the ears. The antlers are branched.

BABIES: A fawn is born in late spring in a well-protected spot. The mother does not let any other animal near her baby until it is strong enough to keep up with the herd.

FOOD: Grass and leaves.

HABITS: Axis deer live in herds with hundreds of other deer. This animal does not overgraze the grasslands because predators, such as the leopard and wild dog, keep them on the move. Feeding time is usually 4 hours after sunrise and 2 hours before sunset. During the heat of the day the axis rests or goes to a nearby stream for water. They are good swimmers.

RETICULATED GIRAFFE

HOME: Dry, scrubby savanna regions of northern Kenya and Ethiopia in Africa.

LIFE SPAN: 25 years.

LOOKS: The giraffe is the tallest land animal. The male grows three times taller than a human being. It weighs between 1200 and 2800 pounds; the female is smaller. The long, slender but strong neck contains only seven vertebrae, the same as a human. Giraffes have a keen sense of sight, hearing, and smell. This helps them find food or to see danger that is near.

BABIES: A calf is born away from the herd. At birth it is dropped by its mother from a standing position. A newborn measures 6 feet tall and weighs 150 pounds, about the size of a grown man.

FOOD: Branches and leaves of mimosa and acacia trees. Giraffes can go for weeks without drinking water. The leaves they eat give them enough moisture.

HABITS: Giraffes live in herds numbering 12 to 15 members. When danger is near giraffes can run up to 35 miles per hour. To protect themselves they kick with front feet and sometimes use their necks, heads, and horns. When drinking they must spread their front legs wide apart and bend down to lap the water. This position leaves them vulnerable to predators. They sleep standing up because of this, too.

ROCKY MOUNTAIN GOAT

HOME: High mountains above the tree line on rocky crags near snow in the Rocky Mountains and coastal ranges of North America.

LIFE SPAN: 12 to 18 years.

LOOKS: The mountain goat is actually an antelope that looks like a goat and is about the size of a large sheep. Males are larger than females. They have long, thick, white fur, a beard, and short, black, cone-shaped horns 9 inches long. Their hooves have a hard, sharp rim that helps them climb on rocks. The eyes are high on the head, and the ears are narrow.

BABIES: Usually one or two kids are born in late spring. The offspring are able to stand and jump within minutes of birth.

FOOD: Grasses, lichens, shrubs, and trees.

HABITS: Mountain goats are daytime grazers and browsers. In summer they seek out salt in rocks. When winter snows are too deep, they find shelter in caves. Deep snow and snow slides are the greatest danger. Cougars, wolves, bears, and golden eagles prey on the young.

AMERICAN BISON

HOME: Protected parks and refuges in the United States and Canada today.

LIFE SPAN: 20 to 25 years.

LOOKS: There are two kinds of American bison. The Plains bison, found on the Great Plains of the United States, is smaller and lighter in color than the wood bison of Canada. Bison measure 6 feet or more at the shoulder and weigh up to 1½ tons; about the size of a pickup truck. The forelegs are larger and more powerful than the hindlegs. Adults have broad foreheads with two short, curving horns.

BABIES: A calf weighs 40 pounds at birth and within a year grows to 400 pounds. The offspring stay with their mother until they are 3 years old.

FOOD: Grasses, leaves, and small branches, and in winter when food is scarce, mosses and lichens.

HABITS: At one time bison were the main source of food for many Native American peoples. Today herds of 100 or less live in protected reserves. The bison's main predator is the wolf. Adults form a ring around their young and use their heads to hook the enemy and toss them high in the air. Bison are known to be curious and friendly by nature.

BRINDLED WILDEBEEST or GNU

HOME: Plains and surrounding bush of East and South Africa.

LIFE SPAN: 20 years.

LOOKS: The wildebeest is an antelope with a cowlike appearance. They weigh 450 pounds or more; the females are smaller. The head and neck are thick, with long hair on the muzzle and mane and a fringe on the throat. The horns curve forward. The tail is long; the feet are hoofed.

BABIES: A well-developed calf is born in January or February when there is plenty of grass to eat. Within 5 minutes of birth, calves are able to follow their mothers. At this time they are most vulnerable to predators.

FOOD: New grass.

HABITS: Wildebeests are known to feed in the early morning and late afternoon. They like to run, gallop, and kick up their heels in a playful way. Lions, cheetahs, leopards, hyenas, and wild dogs are predators.

BLACK-TAILED PRAIRIE DOG

HOME: Prairies and great plains of western and southwestern United States.

LIFE SPAN: 10 to 11 years.

LOOKS: The prairie dog is slightly larger than a squirrel; the females are smaller than the male. Its body is fat and pear-shaped. The fur is short, coarse, and buff-colored, with a white underside and a black-tipped tail.

BABIES: Two to four young are born in a burrow deep in the ground. The offspring are born hairless and blind. Their eyes open at 5 weeks.

FOOD: Grass, vegetation, and insects.

HABITS: Prairie dogs live in large colonies or towns. Their burrows are from 12 to 100 feet long and down to 14 feet into the ground. A mound of soil marks the entrance and exit openings of the tunnels. Prairie dogs are active during the day. They sit upright, acting as a lookout for predators, such as hawks, coyotes, and badgers. When danger is near they make a high-pitched warning whistle.

NORTH AMERICAN/ CANADIAN PORCUPINE

HOME: Wooded areas of North America.

LIFE SPAN: 10 to 17 years.

LOOKS: Adults grow to 3 feet long and weigh 12 to 30 pounds. This animal is a member of the same family as mice. A porcupine's body is covered with quills, like needles, which are 3 to 4 inches long. Its eyesight is poor; its sense of hearing, smell, and touch is good.

BABIES: The baby's eyes are open at birth, and it can walk.

FOOD: Wood, inner bark of trees, buds of plants, and small twigs.

HABITS: Porcupines live in the trees and are more active at night. When threatened, they raise their quills in defense.

CHINCHILLA

HOME: Burrows and rocks of high mountains in South America.

LIFE SPAN: 4 to 5 years.

LOOKS: The chinchilla is related to the guinea pig. The females are larger than the males. Its fur is soft and dense.

BABIES: Litters consist of five or six young. The offspring are born fully developed with eyes open and a coat of fur.

FOOD: Grasses and herbs.

HABITS: Chinchillas live in groups in burrows or among rocks.

EUROPEAN HEDGEHOG

HOME: Bushes and hedges of Europe, North Africa, New Zealand, and Japan.

LIFE SPAN: 6 to 10 years.

LOOKS: The hedgehog looks like a football covered with sharp spines. It weighs 2½ to 3 pounds. The body has short, powerful legs and strong claws used for digging.

BABIES: Two litters of four to seven babies are born in a year. At 3 weeks after birth the babies accompany the mother out of the nest. Newborns have soft spines that harden within a few days.

FOOD: Insects, worms, slugs, birds' eggs, snails, lizards, frogs, rats, snakes, mice, fruits, and roots.

HABITS: It is active at night. Usually moving slowly, it can run quickly if needed. For protection, the hedgehog rolls into a tight ball, pulling its skin around the body, and then tucks its head and feet inside. Its sharp spines cover the entire body. In colder climates it hibernates in a nest of dry leaves.

GIANT ANTEATER

HOME: Swamps and open forests of South and Central America.

LIFE SPAN: 12 to 14 years.

LOOKS: The giant anteater can grow to the size of a large dog but has long bristly hair. Its tongue pokes out of a small opening at the end of the muzzle when feeding. Anteaters are toothless.

FOOD: Ants, termites, and larvae.

BABIES: The mother anteater carries her baby on her back for a year.

HABITS: Giant anteaters live on the ground and can swim or climb trees if necessary. They can eat 30,000 termites in 1 day.

NINE-BANDED ARMADILLO

HOME: Dense shady cover in southern United States and south to Argentina.

LIFE SPAN: 4 years.

LOOKS: A covering of bony plates protects its back and sides. Armadillos have a good sense of smell. This helps them find food.

BABIES: A litter of four identical young of the same sex is born. The skin of the babies is soft like glove leather at birth but hardens in a few days.

FOOD: Insects, small animals, lizards, roots, dead animals, and eggs.

HABITS: Armadillos live alone or in groups of all the same sex. They hunt at night and are good swimmers.

KOALA

HOME: Eucalyptus forests of Australia.

LIFE SPAN: 12 years.

LOOKS: A koala can weigh up to 35 pounds and be the size of a duffel bag. The body is stocky with a little tail. The large round head has a short muzzle, thick hairy ears, and a large black nose tip. Cheek pouches are used for storing food. All the toes have sharp claws. The female has a brood pouch where she keeps new babies. Koalas are marsupials.

BABIES: A baby is the size of a peanut at birth. It crawls to the mother's pouch, where it develops for 6 months. It grows to 7 inches long. After leaving the pouch the furry offspring rides on the mother's back for 3 months.

FOOD: Tender shoots of eucalyptus.

HABITS: Koalas are awake at night and sleep during the day in a forked tree branch. They come to the ground only when they cannot jump to the next tree.

GREAT GRAY KANGAROO

HOME: Plains, woodlands, and forests of Australia and Tasmania.

LIFE SPAN: 10 to 15 years in the wild; 28 years in the zoo.

LOOKS: The kangaroo has a small deerlike head with large ears. It has a small chest and small front legs. A kangaroo has large, strong hindlegs. Its long thick tail is used as a "third leg" when standing up. The male weighs 200 pounds; the female is smaller. Kangaroos have a good sense of sight, hearing, and smell. The kangaroo is a marsupial.

BABIES: A baby or "joey" is born blind and hairless. It's about the size of your thumb. The newborn crawls up to the mother's pouch, where it is fed and kept warm. In a few months it is big enough to leave the pouch and hop on the ground.

FOOD: Grass and other plants.

HABITS: Kangaroos live in groups called mobs. They eat in early morning or just before dark. During the day they nap or groom themselves. Kangaroos can run 40 miles per hour for short distances jump over 5 foot fences, and make 30 foot leaps.

AMERICAN ALLIGATOR

HOME: Swamps, rivers, and lakes of the southern part of North America.

LIFE SPAN: 50 years.

LOOKS: The adult grows to a length of 5 to 20 feet. Its ears, eyes, and nose are on the top of the head, so the alligator can hear, see, and breathe while its body is under water. An alligator's head is wider, shorter, and blunter than a crocodile's.

BABIES: Baby alligators are born fully developed and are about the size of a banana. They are able to swim.

FOOD: Fish, frogs, snakes, waterbirds, and small animals.

HABITS: Alligators spend most of their time sunning themselves on the banks of rivers. When annoyed, the males open their jaws wide and roar.

NILE CROCODILE

HOME: Rivers and pools of water in Africa.

LIFE SPAN: 50 years.

LOOKS: The crocodile is about the same size as an alligator. Its teeth are in even rows, unlike the alligator's. It is cold-blooded.

BABIES: A nest is built on land to hatch eggs. The mother crocodile guards this nest until her babies are hatched.

FOOD: Fish, birds, and small animals.

HABITS: Crocodiles come out of the water early in the day to warm their bodies and return to the water late in the afternoon to cool themselves.

BOA CONSTRICTOR

HOME: Dry warm regions; tropics in Mexico south to Argentina and some islands.

LIFE SPAN: 40 years.

LOOKS: An adult can grow as long as a car. A special pattern on the body helps the snake look like its surroundings.

BABIES: A nest of 20 to 60 young are born live. At birth they are about as long as a rolling pin, or 18 inches. The length doubles in 1 year.

FOOD: Birds and various small mammals, such as rodents.

HABITS: The boa constrictor is a night hunter. It is shy and quiet. This snake kills its prey by wrapping tightly around the victim to suffocate it. Then the prey is swallowed whole, usually head first.

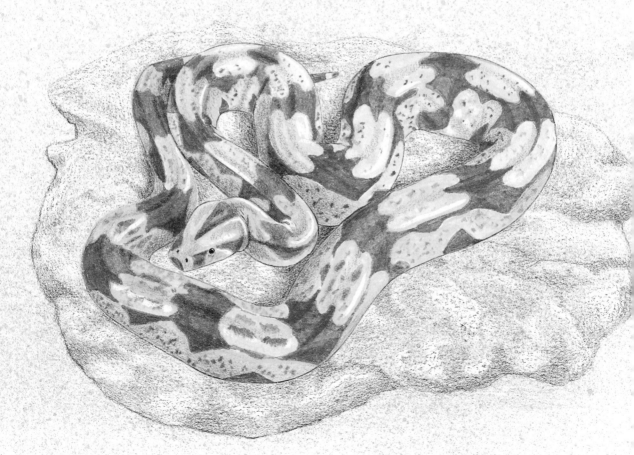

GREEN IGUANA

HOME: Tropical regions of southern Mexico south to Brazil.

LIFE SPAN: 10 years.

LOOKS: Large adults have grown to 7 feet, about the length of a bed. The iguana looks like a small, scaled dragon.

BABIES: The offspring hatch from eggs. They are as long as a grown man's shoe or about 10 inches. By 1 year of age they grow to 3 feet.

FOOD: Babies eat insects, snails, and worms; adults eat plants.

HABITS: The green iguana lives in trees. It likes to live near a river, where it swims. It also hides in the water.

GALAPAGOS TORTOISE

ENDANGERED SPECIES

HOME: Cool, moist forests to dry lands of the Galapagos Islands.

LIFE SPAN: 100 years or more.

LOOKS: There are nine kinds of Galapagos tortoise. The adults weigh up to 500 pounds and can grow bigger than a wheelbarrow. The shell is thick and heavy. Each foot has four claws. You can tell the difference between males and females by the underside of their shells. Females have a flat underside; the shells are curved inward on the males. The difference in shape helps them fit together when they mate.

BABIES: The female lays 2 to 17 golfball-sized eggs in a 12 inch deep pit she digs with her back feet. After all the eggs are laid, they are covered with damp soil and the female leaves. When hatched, the fully developed young dig themselves out of the pit. They can feed and care for themselves without adult help.

FOOD: Almost any plants, even cactus!

HABITS: The male is territorial. He keeps this area to himself by showing how high he can raise his head. The tortoise that can raise its head the highest is considered the strongest. Females wander anywhere they can find food.

FLAMINGO

HOME: In and near shallow brackish or salt water in warm climates.

LIFE SPAN: 25 years in the wild; 50 years in the zoo.

LOOKS: The neck and legs of a flamingo are long. It has an unusual bill that is bent downward. The knees bend backward.

BABIES: The gray chick can swim within 1 week after hatching. It is able to feed and care for itself within 3 weeks. By 2 years of age it has pink and white feathers.

FOOD: Small parts of plants and tiny water animals; sometimes insects.

HABITS: Flamingos are friendly and can be found in large flocks.

KEEL-BILLED TOUCAN

HOME: Wooded savannas, rain forests, plains, and mountains of Mexico through northern Argentina.

LIFE SPAN: 10 to 20 years.

LOOKS: It has a large, colorful bill that is honeycombed to make it light in weight. The bill has sharp knifelike edges for breaking off food. The feet enable it to perch on branches. The beak and feathers are colorful.

BABIES: Both male and female take turns sitting on eggs. The chicks are blind and helpless when hatched.

FOOD: Fleshy sweet fruit, insects, and eggs of other birds.

HABITS: To feed itself, the toucan must tear off food and toss it into the air, catching it in its open beak.

OSTRICH

HOME: Desert and bush regions of Africa and Australia.

LIFE SPAN: 15 or more years.

LOOKS: The ostrich is the largest living bird. It grows taller than a door and can weigh as much as 300 pounds. Its head is small, with large eyes and long black eyelashes. The neck is long and slender. Its feathers are limited to the body. The males are black with white plumes on the tail and wings; the females are brown. Each foot has two toes with claws. Ostriches cannot fly.

BABIES: The eggs are laid by several females (hens) in a large nest. One female scares the other hens away, and she and the male take turns sitting on the eggs. From 10 to 25 chicks are hatched. Chicks can run almost immediately.

FOOD: Shoots, leaves, seeds, small animals, and succulent plants.

HABITS: Ostriches can run 40 miles an hour and can leap over 10 feet.

MAGELLANIC PENGUIN

HOME: Rocky shores on Atlantic Coast of South America.

LIFE SPAN: 12 to 15 years in the wild; 25 years in the zoo.

LOOKS: An adult is 16 inches tall, as tall as a stack of three peanut butter jars. It weighs about the same as a big housecat. The body is covered with dense feathers. The feet are webbed.

BABIES: Penguins lay eggs. The chick is covered with soft down when hatched. By the age of 2 years, the chicks have adult feathers and are black and white.

FOOD: Squid, small fish, and sardines.

HABITS: Penguins make different sounds, including a moo, a bleat, and a cackle, and they can bray like a donkey.

SNOWY OWL

HOME: Barren treeless lands of the far north of Eurasia and North America and Arctic islands.

LIFE SPAN: 15 to 20 years.

LOOKS: Snowy owls are 20 to 24 inches tall, about the size of a fire hydrant. The females are larger than the males. Good eyesight and hearing help them find food.

BABIES: When the eggs hatch, the female feeds the chicks. At 3 weeks they leave the nest and find shelter in rocks until they can fly.

FOOD: Small animals and birds.

HABITS: Snowy owls hunt from a perch, such as a rock or a fence post. They can fly fast enough to catch birds in flight.

GLOSSARY

Burrow   a hole dug in the ground by an animal to be used for shelter

Calluses   thickened skin

Canine teeth   long sharp teeth in the front part of mouth that are used for biting and tearing

Den   a shelter used for sleeping, giving birth, and raising young

Forelegs   front legs of an animal

Graze   to feed on grasses or low-growing plants

Litter   several babies at birth

Marsupial   animals with a pouch in which babies develop

Offspring   babies

Pouch   a pocketlike sac on an animal

Predator   an animal that hunts other animals to kill for food

Prey   an animal hunted and/or killed by another animal

Rodent   a group (order) of animals that includes rats, mice, squirrels, and porcupines

Savanna   a flat, treeless open area or grassland

Scavenge   to gather garbage or decaying matter

Stalk   a slow stiff walk while following prey

Succulent   full of moisture

Tundra   cold treeless area of the Arctic

Vegetation   plants

Wean   to slowly stop giving a baby its mother's milk

Wild (n)   natural state in nature; not domesticated or in captivity